FLORENCE

Designed and Produced by

Ted Smart & David Gibbon

MAYFLOWER BOOKS · NEW YORK CITY

THE anglicized name for the city of Firenze conjures up visions of Victorian ladies sketching in the olive groves, of hansom cab drives among the vineyards and ecstatic sighs before the paintings of Fra Angelico and Botticelli, the two artists who more than any others expressed the romantic view of Florence beloved by the 19th century tourist. In their works all is sweetness and light, and the glory of their genius is pure and far removed from worldly corruption. Theirs is an ideal world, the world all people of good will strive for but rarely attain, so it is appropriate that they should represent one side of the spiritual life of a city which was the cradle of modern, western civilization. The other, darker side is apparent in the work of Pollaiulo and Michelangelo, which contains an ominous sense of violence and doom.

These two sides of the Florentine soul are visible even to the present-day visitor, and it is their constant presence that leaves a longlasting and powerful imprint on his sensibility. On the one hand are the green hills of Fiesole in the spring time, the Boboli Gardens, and the gem-like Church of San Miniato with its marble facings, on the hill above the Belvedere; on the other are the fortress-like palazzi of the Medicis, Strozzis and Spini Ferroni which dominate the city center, and the austere Piazza della Signoria with its Loggia, the statues of which include Perseus holding aloft the bleeding head of the Medusa, the Rape of the Sabine women, and Menelaus holding the dying body of Patroclus. Even today a night-time stroll in the narrow streets can revive images of many murders and other crimes committed in them while poets sang and artists painted in the halls of the buildings above.

Past and present merging in Florence give it a never-ending mystery and attraction. The city has not changed fundamentally in five hundred years, and in its stones are buried the echoes of clashing swords, the cries of victims, the clatter of horses' hooves, shouts of 'Tyrant', 'Traitor' and 'Assassin', and the crackle of the fires which destroyed palaces and brought to an end the extraordinary rule of the monk Savonarola.

From Fiesole, where the Etruscans built a city which the Romans enlarged, turning it into one of their standard provincial outposts, complete with amphitheater and basilica, there is a fine view of Florence. Over the olive-covered slopes the eye slips down into the broad valley of the Arno, and there in the center is the ocher smudge of the city that, more than any other, is the source of the intellectual concepts on which modern European ideas and philosophies are founded. Free enterprise, profitability and democratic government were the often-unfulfilled aims of the Florentine Republic. To these one should add survival, for the tangled thread of family intrigue and Machiavellian

Beneath the shadowy bridge left flow the burnished waters of the Arno River, turned to a sea of molten gold by a heavy sun that hangs suspended as day gives way to night.

diplomacy makes sense only when it is seen in the context of the intricate pattern by which Florence survived and became great in the dangerous world of the early centuries of modern Europe.

Seen from Fiesole, Florence appears as a kind of oasis in a vast and empty valley: in its early years a desolate valley offering little shelter or comfort to the travelers who used it as a halfway house as they made their way from the domains of the Pope across the Appenines into Lombardy and from there up the alpine valleys connecting Italy with the trading centers of northern Europe.

Many of these travelers were traders engaged in the import and export businesses of a Europe only lately developing its trade in wool and cloth, and who looked towards the east for their silks, spices and other luxury goods. Others were scholars bound for the centers of learning at Aachen, in Paris, or across the Channel in Oxford. They carried with them, like the burs they picked up as they walked over the grassy hills, new ideas which would bring about a rebirth of thought to sweep away all trace of the rigid forms of life of feudal Europe. Florence was an important stopping place on their journey and a suitable place in which to transact business. From its earliest days as a modern city, Florence was able to meet its visitors' demands for banking services. The city provided letters of credit, bank drafts and loans to traders and – more importantly – to barons and kings whose territorial ambitions required financing and whose success in these matters meant not only interest earned but also an increase in the sphere of influence for the eighty banks operating in Florence. Success, however, was not inevitable: the failure of Edward III of England to achieve his dreams of European domination brought ruin to the banking houses of Bardi and Ferruzzi when he could not repay the loans they had made to him.

Even today, looking from Fiesole, it is easy to imagine the caravans of business men and scholars making their way in and out of the 14th century city which was already beginning to acquire those monuments which make it so easy to pick out on the earth-coloured plain. The Cathedral of Santa Maria del Fiore had been started by Arnolfo di Cambio in 1296, though that work of genius, the Brunelleschi dome, was not completed until 1434. The Giotto tower had been started, the Badia built and the Bargello Palace was being used as the headquarters of the Captain of Justice of the city.

The panoramic view from the crest of the hills which border the valley no doubt raised in those early travelers the sense of well-being and calm anticipation common to all travelers whose destination comes into view. In winter the hills would have a powdering of snow and the leafless poplars and fruit trees would stand silhouetted against the landscape; in spring the flower-covered meadows which inspired Fra Angelico and Botticelli would heighten the sense of excitement at reaching the city; in summer and autumn the dull ochers and grays of the buildings would merge into the dry landscape. It would be hard to believe that this calm countryside was, in fact, the setting for frenzied and ruthless political maneuverings where families struggled against families, cities against cities and the pope's followers, the Guelphs, against those of the Emperors of the Holy Roman Empire, the Ghibellines.

The origins of the situation in which the Florentines found themselves lay in the collapse of the Roman system of civilization which, sinking into unimaginative and obstructive bureaucracy, was ripe for infiltration by more dynamic but less instructed peoples, uninterested in stemming the slow disintegration of the former culture. Efforts to preserve the tottering remnants of the Roman system in Byzantium, or to recreate it as the Holy Roman Empire, were stopgaps, and Europe continued without a unifying principle until the Italian Renaissance gave it the lead it was looking for.

Various factors gave Italy this unique place in the history of modern Europe. She was the seat of Christianity, the only unifying principle that had sustained Europe through the dark ages, she was well situated on the trading routes between east and west, she had an extensive coastline which encouraged the development of maritime communication and she was free of domination by a great power. The papal domains, though spiritually powerful, never attained the military and administrative dominance of the northern kingdoms.

In these circumstances, the spirit of free enterprise blossomed freely, with opportunities for all. The centers of power were the families who ran feudal courts, and kept the loyalty of their supporters by handing out lands, titles, business concessions and other rewards. In each city, there rose and grew in power such families as the Visconti of Milan, the Scaligeri of Verona, the Este of Ferrara, the Farnese and Borgias of Rome and the Medici of Florence.

Though it is the Medici name which is most closely associated with power in Florence, the family did not have things entirely their own way. A walk through the center of Florence today takes one past the houses of the Medicis' rivals standing like fortresses amid the bustling traffic. At the corner of Via Tornabuoni stands the Strozzi Palace; on the south bank of the river, the Pitti Palace, and in Piazza Trinita the Palazzo Ferroni, with its crenelated silhouette. Of the Pazzi, archrivals of the Medici, who were wiped out after an abortive takeover in which Lorenzo the Magnificent's brother was killed while attending Mass, there are few signs, however.

To survive in those unruly, free-for-all days, one had to be decisive and ruthless, as Dante found out when he was exiled in 1302, after the Pope called on Charles of Anjou's help to drive out the White, and more liberal, political party and installed the tyrannical Corso Donati to rule the city and keep it firmly in the Papal camp. At that time, the power of the Medicis was just beginning. They had become successful businessmen and bankers and already played a part in governing the city. Their success was their undoing and, in the early days, they were imprisoned by jealous rivals and would have been killed except that they were able to bribe their way into exile.

But money was power in Florence, and soon the Medici's first great chief, Cosimo, was ruling Florence again. This time the family held on to power for several generations though they had a close call when the Pazzi family, whom they themselves had exiled, attempted to murder them during Mass.

The Medicis never really recovered from the Pazzi plot of 1478. In one terrible morning they suddenly saw everything that they had striven for hang in the balance as Francesco Pazzi and his friends drew their daggers at the moment of the Elevation of the Host and stabbed Giuliano Medici to death. His brother Lorenzo the Magnificent barely escaped with his life. A dagger caught him in the neck but he drew his sword and, defending himself with his cape, made his escape through the doors of the sacristy. Francesco Nori, one of the Medici bankers, threw himself between Lorenzo and his would-be killers, giving him time to get away, but was killed himself.

By this time, the whole cathedral was in an uproar. Medici supporters jumped over the pews to attack the Pazzi gang and there was some confusion about whether Cardinal Raffaello, who had been conducting the service, was one of the conspirators. Meanwhile, the real plotter, Archbishop Salviati, had arrived at the Palazzo Vecchio with a band of Perugians and the bell of the somber fortress tolled to summon the populace to take arms against the Medici.

In the ensuing street battles between the rival bands of supporters the tide turned in favor of Lorenzo. The Archbishop and Francesco Pazzi were captured and hanged from the upper story of the Palazzo. Lorenzo, having stopped the flow of blood from his wound, addressed the people asking them to restrain their passion for vengeance. Like Mark Antony's speech after the death of Julius Caesar, this only inflamed the mob further and before the end of the day the death of Giuliano was avenged by the slaughter of eighty of the Pazzi and their supporters, and the second most famous banking family of Florence ceased to exist.

For Lorenzo, the plot, though ensuring his position and that of his family, was a hard lesson in the perils of leadership. It soon became evident that the whole conspiracy had been planned over a long period with the collusion of Pope Sextus IV who had coveted the city of Florence for his own domains and who, with King Ferdinand of Naples, had planned to crush the power of the city. Public reaction to the failure of the plot was overwhelming, strengthening Florentine pride and uniting everyone under the Medici Banner.

An even less expected danger to the Medicis came fourteen years later, in 1492, when the Dominican monk

Savonarola arrived in Florence. Lorenzo was fatally ill at the time and was unable to comprehend the danger the fanatical monk presented to the state. He agreed to allow Savonarola to lecture at the Convent of San Marco, the same one which had been decorated by Fra Angelico under the patronage of Cosimo Medici. Savonarola soon inflamed the public with his doomsday rhetoric. Meanwhile Lorenzo died and his weak and incompetent son Piero was exiled.

The monk had arrived at a hiatus in Florentine politics and he now appeared to the people as a new leader, denouncing vice and threatening the proud and the mighty with damnation in the hereafter. Incredible as it may seem, he won the people over and strengthened his claim to their allegiance by defying the King of France, who at that time was traveling through Italy on his way to establish a claim to the Kingdom of Naples. Savonarola's success in persuading the King to consider his spiritual health and to leave Florence unharmed confirmed him in the public mind as a worthy ruler of the city. Savonarola's triumph was shortlived, however, and he soon discovered that ruling Florence was not as easy as arousing the emotions of its inhabitants. Moreover, Savonarola made an enemy of Alexander VI, the Borgia Pope whose election had been supported by the Medicis.

After a series of events, more in the nature of commedia del arte than politics, and which involved a challenge to Savonarola to prove the truth of his doctrines by walking through fire, the monk was seized at his headquarters in the Convent of San Marco. After several days of torture on the rack, he recanted and was sentenced to death by hanging. Immediately after the hanging, Savonarola's body was burned in the piazza before the Palazzo Vecchio.

With the death of Savonarola there came a period of calm to the turbulent city, though it still continued to defy papal authority. When Alexander died he was followed by Julius II, a warlike Pope dedicated to throwing the French out of Italy and restoring the papal influence in the chief cities. With his support, the Medicis reappeared before the gates of Florence on September 1, 1512, and were received with joy by the aristocratic party.

The Medici power, and indeed the Florentine Republic itself, was on the wane however. Wars had drained the resources of the treasury; bankers in Rome, Milan and other parts of Europe were challenging the Florentine supremacy in business and America had been discovered. On the surface, Florentine power still appeared impressive. Cultural life, which had been given its impulse by Lorenzo, flourished and the genius of the city's inhabitants still produced new ideas and innovations in the arts.

Among the brilliant young men of the day was Niccolo Machiavelli, son of an impoverished noble family, who had served as an invaluable ambassador in the Courts of Rome, France and Germany. As a result of his journeys and his experiences, he gained an insight into the workings of political life and he put this to good use in his classic work *The Prince.* In this book Machiavelli summed up for posterity the rules by which the princes of Renaissance Italy lived. It was a survival guide for his time and its truths are timeless. In a way, it was even a prophetic book, for after the corrupt and licentious rule of Alessandro de Medici, there arrived on the scene Duke Cosimo who put into practice Machiavelli's advice to ambitious princes.

Despite its slow extinction as a financial power and source of intellectual life, Florence continued to grow, its buildings increasing in size and impressiveness. The Medici family moved into the vast and imposing edifice of the present-day Palazzo Vecchio and the Duke ordered Vasari to build the palace that now houses the paintings of the Uffizi gallery. The Pitti Palace was completed and the city spread across the river and up into the hills of Fiesole.

As today, however, the confines of the central city remained much as they had been set down, when the Romans first founded their city on the banks of the Arno. The center of this is the area between the cathedral and the river, where there is little trace of ancient Rome except in the general ground plan of the city. Where the forum once stood is now the great square of the Piazza della Republica, surrounded by solid stone buildings erected in the 19th century. Despite its attempt at impressiveness, this is the most characterless area of the city. In the center the parked cars stand in motionless ranks like metal cattle; from the surrounding arcades jut out rows of seats that are filled all day long by tourists, and on summer nights by Florentines as well, sipping their coffees and wines to the accompaniment of combos projecting the latest songs over electronic systems that seem always slightly out of sync.

The amphitheater, which was a distinctive feature of all Roman towns, was near where the Palazzo Vecchio rises in austere majesty over the Piazza della Signoria. There is no trace of it now, though the grid system of the narrow streets reveals a Roman origin, and the curving Via Bentaccordi follows the arc of the arena.

The Piazza is the essence of Medicean Florence. Though the Medicis did not move there until the 16th century it has been in existence since the 13th. To the visitors who crowd the cafés across the square, the huge cliff of brown granite, with its crenelated edge, behind which rises the 94-meter tower, is the most potent of Florentine images. It is a symbol of supreme power and its vastness dwarfs Michelangelo's *David* and the *Neptune* fountain by Ammanati which stand before it. To the right of the palace is the Loggia which, though large and reaching almost half way up the façade of the palazzo, is elegant and light in feeling.

Over to the left, the towers of the Badia and the Bargello peer over the brick tile roofs of Medicean houses in front of which rows of horse carriages wait patiently for passengers while their drivers argue and read the Cronaca di Firenze. Before them stands the equestrian statue of

Cosimo and of the Marzocco, the strange, lion-like beast which is the symbol of Florence.

The great treeless open space of the Piazza della Signoria is a stage on which the dramas of Florentine life are acted out. Here the people have always gathered to voice their opinions or to express their support or disapproval of their leaders. In it and in the surrounding streets crowds have surged, carrying torches and shouting out the Medici rallying cry, 'Palle, Palle', a reference to the symbols of the Medicean coat of arms. In modern times the traditional Florentine football game is played on the square in historic costume and the shouts of the crowd in support of their respective teams echo from the Palazzo walls.

When Savonarola was hanged and burned in the center of the square there was silence. Florentines must have felt then, as on many occasions in their history when an enemy had marched through their gates, or some major assassination had taken place, a sense of unease at the reminder of the narrow gap between life and death, success and failure.

The statues that grace the square are more than mere decorative art objects, and most of them were created to bring home some point that Florence's rulers wanted to impress on their subjects. Like the frescoes in the churches, they were the Renaissance form of today's newspapers and television, a medium through which the public could be brought to consider aspects of political and public life. Donatello's *Judith and Holofernes* which stands by *David* was installed by the speakers' platform from which the rulers of Florence made proclamations or harangued their subjects; the platform was in fact called the *arienghera*. Cellini's splendid *Perseus and the Medusa* was ordered by Duke Cosimo on the return of the Medicis to Florence, after the assassination of Alexander Medici, as a warning to those who might attempt to challenge Medicean power, which was now allied to Rome.

Dominating the whole scene is the *Neptune* which stands surrounded by bronze nymphs and seahorses, in the center of the fountain. This was sculpted by the unfortunate Bartolommeo Ammanati whose work has been the butt of Florentine contempt for centuries because, coming as he did after Michelangelo, his work seems a feeble imitation of the heroic Baroque manner. A contemporary made the remark which has damned the statue: 'Ammanati. Ammanati, che bel marmo hai rovinato'. ('Ammanati what a beautiful piece of marble you have ruined?') Though the 'big white man', as the Florentines call the marble figure, is not a success, the bronzes which surround him give everyone who sees them great pleasure, though there is some doubt whether Ammanati actually sculpted them.

In its early days, Florence was not built down to the river because of the danger, still present, of flooding. In fact, the original bridge across the Arno at its narrowest point in the city, was washed away in 1333, and the present Ponte Vecchio was built in 1345. The silversmiths' and jewelers' shops on it, which are such an attraction to visitors, were once used by butchers and it was Duke Cosimo who ruled that the occupants should follow a more glamorous trade.

Ponte Vecchio is one of the most enchanting features of tourist Florence, with the crowds that move constantly back and forth, examining the wares of shopkeepers and street peddlers who spread their goods on the sidewalk, forming a moving pattern of life and color. At night, the bridge is a haven from the roaring motorbikes and cars that race along the banks of the Arno. Even if the noise of the frenetic Florentine drivers is only mildly diminished, at least the sense of isolation from the rest of the turbulent city is welcome.

Above the Ponte Vecchio runs the covered corridor which joins the Uffizi to the Pitti Palace. This passageway running above the roofs of the houses is the equivalent of what in other cities would be secret passages linking royal houses. Here in Florence the passage flaunts itself but is still wellprotected as it runs its angular course way above street level.

The Uffizi, stretching from the river to the Palazzo Vecchio was, as the name suggests, an office block built to serve the needs of the government. Duke Cosimo commissioned its design from Giorgio Vasari, whose name is best remembered by his book on the lives of the artists of the Italian Renaissance, most of whom were his contemporaries.

Vasari's building was soon filled with the works of art collected by the Medici princes, becoming a great storehouse of the work of the people he had written about. The splendid rooms are a perfect setting for one of the world's greatest art collections, and a place where, Vasari's book in hand, the visitor can come face to face with the Florentine painters whose innovations in their own time were as daring as those of Picasso and the School of Paris in the 20th century.

The collection begins with Cimabue, who broke away from the hieratic art of Byzantium and introduced figures expressing human emotions. According to Vasari, it was Cimabue who discovered Giotto, a simple shepherd boy drawing on stones as he tended the sheep. This story may be apochryphal, but it makes the point that early Renaissance art was a grass roots business and this gave it a universality that the art springing from the more self-aware and intellectual society which developed later, lacked.

Cimabue's tortured, art-nouveauish lines, which must have seemed very innovative in his time, were developed by Giotto, though he gave his figures a humanity that was new in an art which had previously expressed abstract ideas rather than human feelings. The Tuscan Room of the Uffizi gives a splendid opportunity to compare the styles of Cimabue and Giotto and also of Duccio, the Sienese painter, as all three artists are represented by large paintings of the Madonna.

In an age when schooling was in the hands of the church, many young men entered monasteries in spite of themselves rather than because they had a real vocation.

This was very much the case for the kind of intelligent and sensitive spirits who felt unable to cope with the turbulent life of a Renaissance city like Florence. Fra Angelico, whose work is best seen at the Convent of San Marco, was one of these. Probably of a dreamy, nostalgic nature, he gave his paintings a Gothic rather than a Renaissance quality, as is evident in his work *The Coronation of the Virgin* in the Uffizi. Another monk whose work is exhibited at the Uffizi, but who was of a very different temperament, is Filippo Lippi. His tender but more sensual Madonnas have a similarity that suggests they were modeled on the same lady, perhaps the nun Lucrezia whom he abducted and later was allowed to marry, thanks to the intervention of Lorenzo the Magnificent. The work of their son Filippino may be seen in other rooms of the gallery.

The Renaissance spirit was scientific, and this drove artists to experiment with new ways of expressing visual reality. A study of anatomy and of perspective became an essential part of an artist's technique and no one was more dedicated to their mastery than Paolo Uccello. Curiously enough, Uccello never managed to acquire such facility of line and form as Masaccio, who was his contemporary, but he nevertheless produced some impressive works, among which are his three battle scenes painted for Lorenzo Medici's palazzo. The paintings showing battling horses, forests of lances, archers and men in armor, now live in three European cities, with Florence retaining one of them in the Uffizi gallery.

The preoccupation with naturalism was passed on through Pollaiulo and Verrochio to Leonardo da Vinci, who soon outstripped his teacher. What the others did with enormous effort Leonardo managed to achieve with an ease that belies the concentration that went into his works. In the room in the Uffizi that he shares with the Umbrian School, an early example of Leonardo's work can be seen in *The Baptism,* by Verrochio, to which Leonardo contributed the angel on the left of the painting. Leonardo, though born at Vinci, near Florence, was an artist of a universality that separates him from those more identifiably Florentine. Early in his life he left Florence for Milan to work for Ludovico Il Moro, head of the Sforza family, and when he returned to Florence he offered his work to the dreaded Cesare Borgia. Finally, he worked for Francis I of France and died in that country.

Of the unmistakably Florentine painters, none was more so than Sandro Botticelli, whose sinuous line linked him with Cimabue and whose inspiration in pagan and Christian themes was shared by Michelangelo. Botticelli, however, was no Michelangelo. He remained a decorative painter, while the Baroque giant developed a superb naturalistic style, in which sculpture and painting become inextricably combined.

Though the Uffizi contains the works of many painters, both from Italy and other countries, it is the Florentines who are on their home ground here and the ones who provide that shock of recognition that one also finds in street and market place. These, one suddenly realizes, are the Florentines, the turbulent, sardonic, quick-witted people in whose city past, present and future merge in an endless stream of which they are a part. Outside the stately corridors of the old government offices the tide of Florentine life flows on much as in the paintings inside, and the transition from the art gallery to the courtyard outside and to the Lungarno along which the cars and motorbikes roar is not difficult to assimilate. The street vendors with their stalls full of guide books, postcards, Florentine wooden trays and leather book marks, seem direct descendants of those other peddlers who formerly thronged the court with petitions to present to susceptible servants of the state, while the tourists who gaze in awe and wonder at the stone walls of the Palazzo Vecchio are no different from the travelers who have always flocked to Florence on business and pleasure.

This sense of timelessness is most marked in the streets between the old palace, the Duomo and the Piazza Santa Croce. Here, in narrow alleys hemmed in by unfaced stone walls rising high enough on each side to close out the sun except in the middle of the day, are reminders of the people who made the history of the city. The Pazzi, whose assassination plot failed to unseat the Medicis, had their palace in the Via del Proconsolo, and Dante frequented the street named after him; near the river is the Via dei Neri that recalls the bitter rivalry between the Black and White parties, while the Via Ghibellini appears strangely out of place in a city which was a Guelph supporter of the Pope. Michelangelo lived here, and Cimabue, and Ghiberti, the sculptor of the famous doors on the Baptistery, lived at Borgo Allegri.

In contrast to this maze of narrow streets the Piazza Santa Croce appears as a great arena open to the sky against the multicolored backcloth of the façade of the Santa Croce Church. Like other Florentine churches, this one had its façade finished in the 19th century, but the church itself existed even before it was rebuilt by Arnolfo di Cambio in the 13th century. Santa Croce is full of monuments to the famous who were either buried here or had memorial tombs erected to them. Among them are Galileo, Machiavelli, Michelangelo and Rossini. There are also superb works of art, including chapels decorated by Giotto and his school, and an Annunciation bas relief by Donatello which ranks among the finest sculptures in the world. The interior of the church was laid out by Giorgio Vasari who, though born in Arezzo, studied and worked in Florence.

To the right of the church lies one of the most beautiful Renaissance buildings in Florence, the Pazzi chapel, built by Brunelleschi and decorated by various artists of the period. During the 1966 floods that damaged so many Florentine buildings and works of art, the most famous of Cimabue's crucifixions was submerged in the flood waters here and ruined beyond reasonable restoration, though an attempt has been made to give visitors at least some idea of this important and moving work.

The northern limits of the early city circled the area where the Duomo, or Cathedral of Santa Maria del Fiore, rises monumentally above the dusty, rose-colored rooftops. Close up, the bulk of the great church, topped by Brunnelleschi's vast and elegant dome, is overwhelming. The walls rise like cliffs of colored marble, white from the quarries of Carrara, green from those of Prato, black from Como, and red from the coast of Tuscany. The façade is 19th century, but in the style in which the church was originally conceived. Alongside the church rises the elegant marble tower designed by Giotto from which, though it means a stiff climb, there are superb views of the city and of the dome itself, as well as of the Baptistery which stands before it.

From this vantage point the Duomo's central position in the life of the city is brought home. The traffic swarms about the Baptistery; buses, cars, bicycles, motorbikes and even the occasional donkey cart, more often than not loaded with furniture, flow tumultuously on while the pedestrian weaves his way along the sidewalk or makes sudden and frantic dashes across the street. Around the religious buildings are shops, cafés, pizzerias and ice-cream parlors, all doing a lucrative business with the passerby.

In Medicean times this area was also the center of the city, for the Medici palace is not far away and the Via dei Calzaiuoli, street of the shoemakers, was also the busy thoroughfare connecting the Duomo to the Palazzo Vecchio. The tower itself was a good look-out point and any enemy movement over the hills to the south, behind San Miniato or to the north, beyond Fiesole would instantly have been spotted.

The interior of the Duomo is something of a shock after the gaiety of its exterior; here there is a somberness which reminds one that the Florentines were bankers and, like most bankers, were fundamentally a sober and traditional lot without too much time for the fripperies of fashion that people like the Venetians went in for.

The effect is impressive; a vista 153 meters long stretches from the main door to the apse and rises over 90 meters to the lantern that surmounts the cupola. Rows of columns divide the vast space into three aisles and stained glass windows filter the light. There is little of the decoration that one finds in most cathedrals, though there are monuments that stand out in their isolation. The most moving and forceful of these is without doubt the Michelangelo *Pietà*. This marble carving was carried out by the sculptor when he was seventy-five and has a maturity and strength which reveals the depth of thought one might expect from an intelligent man with a whole lifetime of experience on which to draw.

Michelangelo, who looked more like a broken nosed boxer than most people's idea of a sensitive artist, was a man with a tough and resolute spirit. His genius caught the new humanist spirit exactly and his giant, pagan figures with their powerful and restless bodies, expressed the self-confidence of the new Europe in which, free from the bonds of medieval thinking, man felt in control of his destiny. There are other *Pietà* of Michelangelo in St. Peter's in Rome and in Milan, but this one is particularly moving. According to legend, Michelangelo himself was not satisfied with it and tried to smash it.

The other interesting work of art in this sparsely-decorated cathedral commemorates John Hawkwood, an English mercenary whom the Florentines knew as 'd'Acuto'. His memorial shows him on horseback and is a monotone fresco by Uccello, who has attempted to create the optical illusion of a figure in the round.

The Baptistery in front of the church is one of Florence's oldest buildings and rests on foundations that are at least of Roman origin if not earlier. Its octagonal form, completely covered in marble of various colors both inside and out, is striking and sensitively proportioned. Unfortunately, it is a little lost in the confusion of traffic and the later houses which loom around it. It is the kind of building which deserves the green grass that surrounds the religious buildings at Pisa but it is unlikely to achieve this; in Florence the past has to survive alongside the present.

The two treasures of the Baptistery are the famous Ghiberti doors and, inside, a statue of the *Magdalen* by Donatello. The doors are a tourist attraction and have received world-wide publicity, while the *Magdalen* is often missed; yet it is one of the most moving statues in Florence, if not in the world.

Donatello preceded Michelangelo and his view of the world was very different. He did not have that superb confidence of the Renaissance man: his world was one of suffering and endurance; of ordinary mortals and not supermen. The *Magdalen* is a figure carved in wood, a thin emaciated figure covered in a shaggy goatskin, a figure, like that of the Donatello Baptist in Santa Croce, who comes from an arid land and exists on a bare subsistence. The arms and legs are muscular and bony and the face parched by the hot sun. There is neither despair, self pity, defiance, nor glory in its expression but it arouses an unsentimental compassion that makes it unforgettable.

This was one side of Donatello. The other had a soft sensuousness which is clearly visible in the *David* and the *Amor-Atys*, a chubby cupid draped with erotic belts and transparent trousers. Both sculptures are in the Bargello Museum. Like most artists of his time, Donatello carried out commissions, privately and for the guilds of master craftsmen and traders. His *St. George* was suitably sculpted for the Armorers Guild and his fine equestrian statue of the mercenary condottiere Gattamelata was modeled and cast in bronze for the Venetians who placed it in Padua where it stands today.

There is no better place to browse and look at the

sculpture of Donatello and other Florentine sculptors than in the Bargello Palace in Piazza San Firenze. This gray, castellated building, from which the Captain of Justice maintained law and order, is often missed by tourists and therefore provides a welcome haven from their company. The Palazzo itself was begun nearly half a century before the Palazzo Vecchio, the back of which stands at the other end of the Piazza, and it has a romantically feudal atmosphere, with a courtyard that has the arms of Florence's leading families embedded in its walls and from which an open staircase leads to the upper floors Here, there is a wide, arcaded balcony with a Gothic arched ceiling where the captain and his family no doubt gathered on hot days to gaze down on the life in the courtyard below. Now the balcony is filled with statues as is the hall, formerly used for the General Council. In this space are the Marzocco and other Donatello statues, a little lonely perhaps away from their original settings, but able to be enjoyed free of the hustle and bustle of more popular tourist galleries.

If the ghosts of the Medicis still linger in Florence, one feels that perhaps they are more likely to be found around the Medici-Riccardi Palace rather than among the official buildings of the Piazza della Signoria. The Borgo San Lorenzo, which leads down to the Medici's palace and the Church of San Lorenzo, has that everyday and timeless air of streets that have been markets for generations. There are cafés and pizzerias and rosticcerias from which the rich smells of Florentine beef, turning slowly on a wheel, make the mouth water. Along the sidewalks, stalls packed with clothing, shoes and food stand colorfully crowded together. This is where everyone goes for the bargain pair of shoes made of that marvellously soft leather which the Florentines use, or where housewives buy lace tablecloths, or children's clothes. The Piazza San Lorenzo, by the Church, is the hub of all this activity. Under the sun-bleached canvas of the stalls, gossip, bartering, and arguments go on in time-honored fashion, while the lire notes exchange hands.

Overlooking the Piazza is the Palazzo Medici-Riccardi, originally built by Michelozzo Michelozzi for the old Cosimo, who was the first Medici to rule the city, and acquired by the Riccardis in the 17th century. The interior of the palace is a fine example of the Florentine Renaissance style. In the chapel is a fresco by Bonozzo Gozzoli which is poignantly expressive of the more peaceful side of the life of the Medicis. Although the fresco's subject is ostensibly the *Voyage of the Three Kings,* it is in fact a portrait of the Medici family. The procession shows them with their retainers riding through the rocky Florentine hills where men are hunting deer. In the foreground a young man rides a white horse with fine leather trappings; he is accompanied by young attendants and he wears a hat suggesting a crown – it is Lorenzo the Magnificent as a youth. Behind him rides his father Piero with Cosimo, now an old man. The painting confirms the

youthfulness of the Florentine court and the closeness of the ties that bound the followers of a powerful Renaissance lord. A more macabre relic of the great Lorenzo is his death mask in the Palazzo's museum, in which there are also portraits of the Medicis.

More Medici portraits, this time on their tombs, are across the Piazza at the Medici chapels and tombs alongside the San Lorenzo Church. The most splendid of these, carved by Michelangelo in a New Sacristy designed by him, are dedicated to Giuliano, son of Lorenzo, and to Lorenzo II, his grandson. The figures of the two Medici Dukes are enhanced by two pairs of figures in Michelangelo's most robust Baroque style; they represent Dawn and Dusk, Day and Night, and embody the feeling of a heroic twilight of god-like creatures which infuses Michelangelo's later work.

One of the few churches in Florence that had its façade completed within a few years of being built is that of Santa Maria Novella, which lies not far from San Lorenzo. It is a Dominican church and was built by Jacopo Talenti who set a style for monumental churches in Florence. In front of the church is a piazza with a fountain where Florentines, especially mothers with their children, often gather.

The church itself is as austere as the other Florentine churches but has chapels and monuments which relieve the bare walls, and the apse is covered with paintings by Ghirlandaio. Filippo Strozzi, the Renaissance banker and rival of the Medicis, is buried here. The Spanish Chapel, built in honor of St. Thomas Aquinas, has well-preserved frescoes of the life of the saint.

Today, Santa Maria Novella lies near the railway station in a busy quarter where the traffic of people coming and going is incessant, and inexpensive overnight hotels line the narrow streets. Many of them, like houses all over Florence, have echoes of a more splendid past and fine rooms may have stuccoed ceilings on which frescoes, in imitation of the golden age of Florence, have been attempted. Though not high art, these houses retain some of the atmosphere of old Florence and have considerable charm, though they may lack many of the modern conveniences that travelers demand. No doubt they will gradually be refurbished and modernized with plastic and veneer and something of the old Florence will disappear for ever.

The redevelopment of Florence is, thankfully, a slow process and the attractions of the city remain on the whole those for which the 19th century traveler came. At one time or another the city has played host to almost everyone of note, as well as to thousands who have come and gone, leaving only their name in the hotel register to mark their passing through. Among the famous who cultivated Florence in the past have been Prince Charles Edward Stuart the young Pretender; Princess Mary of Teck, later Queen Mary of England; Mark Twain; and Bernard Berenson, whose dedication to the art of the city opened the world's eyes to the beauties of medieval painters.

It is to savor the glories of Florence's museums and galleries that most people visit the city, but there are still today, as there have been for centuries past, other pleasures to be experienced. One is the continuing tradition of craftsmanship. Florence is still a city of cottage industries and many of the products that carry world-famous names are made by the dexterous fingers of individuals who do the work in small factories or at home.

For the visitor there is endless pleasure to be found in the small shops of the Via Tornabuoni, where dressmakers, glove makers, shoe and antique shops dress their windows with that characteristic Florentine flair for form and understatement.

The Florentine shopkeeper is still an individualist and every transaction becomes a social occasion in which conversation is exchanged as the quality of the article is discussed. The shopkeeper is often personally interested in the style and quality of the goods he or she is selling and this is a welcome change from the manner of shops in large cities. This interest in the business at hand, and in the customer, is an Italian trait which is particularly marked in Florence, perhaps because the experience of centuries of dealing with foreign visitors has heightened the normal Italian interest in other people.

At any rate, it turns the business of shopping in Florence into an entertainment, whether one is concerned with clothes or the old books that are sold around the Piazza del Signoria or the lovely Piazza Annunziata with its colonnaded church and the Spedale degli Innocenti.

For the tourist, Florence produces endless versions of its traditional Florentine work in leather and wood. It is difficult to resist the painted trays, tables, book ends, boxes – musical and silent – albums and other objects, all laid out in the Florence sunshine. The new market on Via Porta Rossa near the Ponte Vecchio is a 16th century loggia among whose columns there are stalls crammed with leather goods, straw goods and embroidery. Outside it, on one of the busiest corners of central Florence, sits a large bronze boar, the snout of which is kept shiny by the hands of those who stroke it for luck.

Many of the workers who produce the goods for this market, as well as for other shops in the city center, live across the Arno in Oltrarno. This quarter stretches from the river to the slopes of the hill where the gardens of the Pitti Palace stretch up to the Belvedere castle which stands astride the city wall.

The city's small workshops are found largely in the Borgo San Frediano, which runs parallel to the river from Piazza Sauro to the western city wall, and which most visitors, dazzled by the attractions on the northern side of the Arno, do not visit. The loss is theirs, for here is the authentic flavor of the life of the working Florentines. Along the streets runs a continual pageant of people and vehicles. Ancient cars piled high with merchandise run alongside the sleek new models of the rich; donkeys on

their thin legs pull incredible loads, and when there is no vehicle available, furniture, washing and baskets of fruit are carried by hand along the streets. The tempo of life seems less relaxed than on the other side of the Arno. Everyone is in a hurry, except those who have nowhere to go, who sit in the entrances to the dusty houses with their broken shutters and decaying plaster.

Off the Borgo is the Church of the Carmine, built in 1268, and possessing one of the most significant series of frescoes in the history of art. They are by Masaccio and are in the Brancacci Chapel, one of the few parts of the church to survive a fire in 1771. Masaccio learned Giotto's lessons and added a sense of solidity and atmosphere to his figures, making them appear more three-dimensional and natural than had ever been done before. The paintings depict scenes from the Old and New Testaments; particularly worthy of note are the scenes showing the collection of the tribute money and St. John healing the sick.

On quite a different scale is the showpiece of Oltrarno, the Pitti Palace, which contains the Palatine collection of works of art. The Palace itself looks forbidding outside, with a vast, gravel-covered open space now used as a parking lot, but it is lavishly decorated with figures and elaborate wood and plaster work painted and gilded in the style which became *de rigeur* among the successful rulers of the 17th century.

The Medicis acquired the palace in 1549 when Eleanor de Toledo, the wife of Duke Cosimo, bought it and had it enlarged by Ammanati, and the gardens laid out by Tribolo. It was presented to the state in 1919 by King Victor Emmanuelle III. The works of art in the Pitti are largely of the 15th and 16th centuries and are mounted in heavy gold frames which all but overpower their contents. There are some fine works of the masters of the High Renaissance: Titian, Tintoretto and Paolo Veronese, whose style satisfied a clientele with more hedonistic tastes than those of the earlier painters' time.

The Pitti expresses the Florentine spirit in decadence. The spare, self-disciplined style of Lorenzo's day has disappeared under an opulent overlay of decoration. The walls and ceilings of rooms are decorated elaborately with flowers, figures, scrolls, musical instruments and other symbols of a self-congratulatory civilization. Well-fed bodies gesture rhetorically in the paintings, and portrait heads are placed on enormous bodies clothed in rich furs and silks, symbolizing power. In the rooms, chandeliers hang like astral fruit in huge clusters and in the gardens artificial grottoes groan under the weight of stone garlands. Perhaps the sculptor Cioli was trying to express his own view of the times when he carved the fat naked dwarf astride a tortoise which stands by the entrance to the gardens.

While the lords and their courts were basking in the sunset glow of a fading life style, most Florentines were carrying on with life as they had always done, caring for the vines that still grow on the hillsides, where clusters of earth-colored buildings have stood for generations, plowing the earth between the olive trees with their pale, wide-horned cattle, making the reed baskets for the wine bottles, carving olive wood furniture, embroidering, tanning leather and cultivating vegetables and flowers.

A strong attachment to the land is a Florentine characteristic and many of the inhabitants of the city have a plot of ground, a small vineyard, an orchard or an olive grove which provides their families with another life from that of the city. The land and its produce create a tie between the members of a family, especially if the land is jointly owned, and at harvest time the work of collecting the fruits of a summer's labor are shared and celebrated by all.

The Medicis had several country houses to which they retired during the summer. One of these is at Villa di Castello, six miles to the north of Florence, which though damaged in World War II retains much of the beauty which made it Lorenzo the Magnificent's favorite resort. Another villa, built by Sangallo, specially for Lorenzo, is at Villa di Poggio a Caiano and yet another, now a nurses' home, is at Careggi. Both Lorenzo and Cosimo died at the latter.

The many villages around Florence are in a sense an extension of the city itself, for they are populated either by people who sell their produce in Florence or by those who drive daily to work there. Fiesole, which has over 15,000 inhabitants, is more than just a satellite village; it was one of the chief towns of that mysterious civilization that we call Etruscan, and the Romans fortified it and built baths, temples and an amphitheater with superb views across the wooded hills.

Up on the Fiesole hills life is peaceful, and the olive groves and pines and the distant vistas, fading into that blue which appears so often in Renaissance art, are easily recognized as the inspiration of the painters. Because of its height above sea level (295 meters) Fiesole has splendid views and its cool air attracts many visitors. In summer it is alive with people strolling about the main street or sitting on the grassy slopes around the amphitheater and the little Monastery of San Francesco, from which there is one of the finest of all views of Florence in the valley below. San Bernardino of Siena occupied one of the cells of the monastery which also possesses a charming 14th-century cloister. Below it lies the Romanesque Duomo, the campanile of which resembles the towers which excessively proud families in Renaissance Italy added to their houses, partly to watch out for enemies but also as a sign of their importance.

To the south of Fiesole lies the Church of San Domenico, where Fra Angelico studied and took his vows. There is a painting of the Madonna by him in one of the chapels, and a crucifixion in the Chapter House.

To the west of Florence, in the valley of the Arno as it flows down to the sea at Pisa, is Prato, the first of the cities of the Arno basin to come under Florentine influence. It was a rich wool city and still holds a commanding position in the Italian textile trade. Among its important monuments is the Duomo, a Romanesque building in which there are frescoes of Fra Filippo Lippi who lived in Prato and who, having been released from his monastic vows in order that he could marry his mistress Lucrezia, continued his amorous way until he was poisoned by a jealous husband. The Church also possesses a sacred relic – a waist sash given to Doubting Thomas by the Virgin to prove her Assumption. The story of the relic is told in frescoes by Agnolo Gaddi, who decorated the chapel in which it lies.

Prato was twice involved in the wars that embroiled Florence; on the first occasion it was the victim of the armies of Naples and the Pope who had marched north in 1512 to support Giovanni and Giuliano Medici after the family had been ousted, following the assassination of the disreputable Alessandro Medici; on the second it became the scene of a battle between the forces of Filippo Strozzi, the banker rival of the Medicis, and the Florentine forces under Duke Cosimo. Strozzi was defeated and his palace confiscated, while he himself was imprisoned and committed suicide.

Pisa, Lucca, San Gimignano and Siena were all rivals of each other and of Florence. Their rivalry took the form not only of armed combat, though this was avoided as often as possible as the mercenary Condottiere and his troops were a drain on the cities' resources, but in vying with each other in the splendor of their buildings and the strength of their fortifications. Around Florence, therefore, there is a constellation of fine towns, each with magnificent buildings and works of art which would enrich any museum.

Fortunately for visitors, museums have not yet snatched away the natural heritage of the Tuscan countryside and its man-made wonders can be enjoyed as part of the whole picture of Tuscany. In Siena, there is a fresco by Simone Martini in the Palazzo Publico which expresses the Tuscan scene precisely. In it, one sees the noble lord Guidoriccio da Gogliano riding across the bare countryside on a horse richly caparisoned, like his master, in a cape with a diamond pattern. Behind him lies a castle and an armed camp, before him a walled city. There is no sign of people in any of the places; Lord Guidoriccio appears to be completely alone as he makes his way towards the city.

It is an impression often felt by travelers today as they drive along a secondary road in the countryside surrounding Florence: the absence of people is quite remarkable. The fields are empty, the olive groves and vineyards unattended, even the white oxen are as motionless as statues. In the villages and clusters of farm buildings on the summits of the hills there is little sign of movement, a rooster may be scratching at the grass between the cobbles or a thin dog sniffing at a pile of rubbish, but the people are absent.

On Sunday, the scene changes. The cafés that were unattended on a weekday are full of people dressed in their

Sunday best and the restaurants are bustling with active waiters shouting their orders or, in summer, scurrying in and out as they serve the customers sitting under the shade of plane trees. Like all Italians, the Florentines make Sunday the day for the family and the children are dressed in their finest and most expensive clothes and are admired and spoiled, though this treatment does not seem to ruin their good manners.

After lunch, the families gather in the piazzas or stroll down tree-shaded avenues. Wherever they gather there are entertainments and food, children's merry-go-rounds sometimes powered by a donkey or, more often, by a small electric motor, ice cream vans and street vendors with their baskets full of candies and biscuits.

The atmosphere of a Sunday is heightened when there is some special festival to celebrate. In Florence, Easter Sunday is both a religious festival and a rite of spring. The focal point of the day's events is the Duomo, where a float covered in flowers is placed outside the west façade, while inside the church the Easter service takes place. At a given moment a dove flies along a wire from the high altar to the decorated car and ignites a firework which makes the car explode, showering the sidewalk around it with flowers while the crowd applauds this symbolic ritual, which seems to represent both the natural rebirth of the year and the renewal of spiritual life.

The Easter Festival is an excuse for enjoying all the good things of life and the shop counters are piled with things to eat. The traditional Palomba, a cake shaped like a dove, is on sale everywhere and if not eaten on the premises is carried home triumphantly in its fancy box, to be shared later by the whole family. Another Easter cake is ring-shaped and has hard-boiled eggs decorating it. There are also piles of the famous nut-packed cakes from Siena called Panforte. In the restaurants, families gather to celebrate the Easter feast, many of them having attended the morning church services, and the lunch-time celebration goes on well into the afternoon.

Following Easter there is the famous Maggio Musicale, a festival of music throughout May, when international orchestras, conductors and soloists gather in the Tuscan city to play in the churches and concert halls. This is a more private occasion than the event that ushers in May and which revives memories of the Medicean years. Surprisingly, this is a football match played in the Boboli Gardens of the Pitti Palace. It is no ordinary match, for the atmosphere is that of the 16th century, and there are processions and side-shows reviving the glory of the days of Duke Cosimo. Later, on the Feast of St. John, in June, the match is replayed before vast crowds at the Piazza della Signoria. The summer festivals come to an end in September with the Rificolona, a parade of old carriages and costumed people carrying lanterns and accompanied by bands and dancers.

Soon after, the tourists begin to disappear and Florence settles down to its normal life, the halls of the Palazzo della Signoria are hushed and the footsteps of art lovers in the Uffizi echo softly in the half-empty corridors. A few of the stall owners in some of the piazzas drift away but the Florentines hardly notice the change; they are used to the comings and goings of strangers. As the air gets cooler and the frost arrives on the hilltops, the towers and campaniles and the great dome of Brunelleschi stand out clearly. From the Piazzale Michelangelo, where a copy of the statue of David stands, staring over the city that he represents so well, the view is stupendous. Down below is the Pitti Palace and beyond it the Oltrarno with its churches and then the river and its bridges. From the Ponte Vecchio the eye moves to the Uffizi and then upwards to the tower of the Palazzo Vecchio, and past it to the Duomo and its attendant towers of the Bargello and Badia.

One can stand for hours on this Piazza, and people do, looking at the city below: it is difficult to fathom its power to hold the attention, and in any case Florence would resist a facile explanation of its charisma. It has never been an introspective city, except perhaps for the brief and un-characteristic period under Savonarola's influence. Its true character is pragmatic and forward-looking. All its buildings and monuments have been the product of people who have looked ahead and they have been created out of strife and argument. When the argument has become too much for the creator he has moved on to something more productive.

When the French arrived at the gates of the city, the Florentines let them in and the invaders soon felt that the temper of the people was against them and they moved on; when the Pazzi tried to murder all the Medicis, Lorenzo begged his followers, in vain, not to exact revenge; when the great condottiere Sforza threatened them, the Florentines bribed him instead of meeting him in useless combat.

Passion and reasonableness, profound faith and lively scepticism make up the paradox of the Florentine spirit and that is the contribution which Florence has made to the formation of the European mind and to the western world of today.

Reflected in the rippled water of the Arno River are the stuccoed walls of the ancient buildings right which line the Ponte Vecchio, the oldest and most famous of the bridges of Florence.

19

At the heart of Florence, in the Piazza del Duomo, are set a group of buildings which are among the most remarkable artistic monuments of the city. Flanked by the soaring bell-tower of Giotto's Campanile below, which rises above the red-tiled roofs of the picturesque buildings previous page that cluster around this ancient square, the Gothic creation of the Cathedral of Santa Maria del Fiore left, the world's third largest church, was begun in 1294 and consecrated in 1436. Capped by Brunelleschi's magnificent dome above, the basilica, with its broad harmonies of colored marble, complements both the Campanile and octagonal Baptistery right.

Built by Neri di Fioravante in 1345, the Ponte Vecchio is pictured overleaf in a further superb view.

24

Beautiful churches, statuary, and time-honored buildings, dominated by the Duomo's Cupola overleaf, are part of the city's rich, artistic tapestry. Shown above is the interior of the Church of Sta. Maria Novella, with its marble decorated façade bottom right; left the interior of the Basilica of San Lorenzo; top right the Basilica of Santa Croce, where lie interred some of the greatest men in the history of Italy; center right the turreted National Museum of The Bargello, and below Giambologna's equestrian statue of the Grand Duke Cosimo 1 de' Medici, which stands in the Piazza della Signoria.

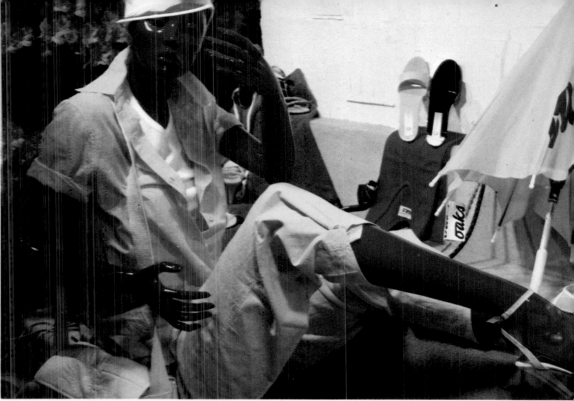

Since the days when the powerful Medici held sway over the city, the pervading Florentine influence, keenly felt in so many spheres – art, architecture, literature and coinage – has extended into the world of fashion, for presenting a 'bella figura' is still today an essential part of the Florentine way of life.

With its history of cloth-making and hand-fashioned crafts, Florence is undoubtedly one of the leaders in haute couture: its beautifully created clothes, supple leather footwear and sophisticated accessories having earned for the city an international reputation for quality and style, and whether displayed in glossy boutiques or 'tucked-away' stores, they are certain to have an irresistible appeal.

Laden stalls crammed with a bewildering variety of merchandise, and ever-popular sidewalk artists who will deftly sketch or paint a portrait *right*, have long been a feature of the bustling street markets at the heart of the city. In the Piazza San Lorenzo, at the center of this popular market, stands Bandinelli's statue of Giovanni delle Bande Nere *above left*, while around the Neptune Fountain in the Piazza della Signoria, with its massive central figure *below*, a troupe of artistes perform before an audience of captivated youngsters *above*. With its row of shops reserved exclusively for goldsmiths, the Ponte Vecchio *left* is particularly enchanting when, floodlit by night *overleaf*, it is reflected in the dark pools of the Arno.

29

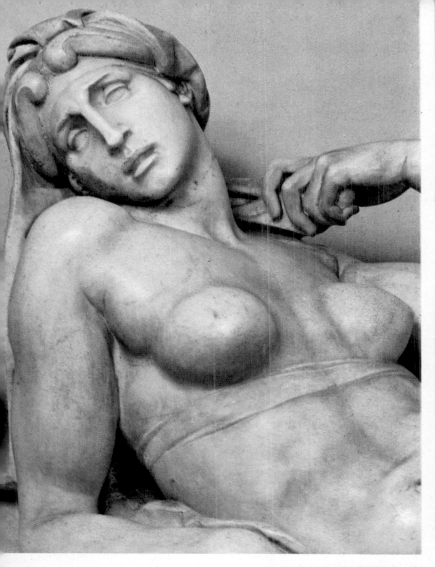

Created by Michelangelo, the statue of David left, which stands in the Gallery of the Academy, was begun by the young artist in 1501 and completed three years later. Carved from a huge block of marble that had been reserved for the purpose since 1462, the work was commissioned by the new Republic of Florence as a symbol of freedom. The gigantic, youthful figure, with its physical loveliness, pride and nobility of expression, reveals how closely Michelangelo adhered to the symbol conceived.

Contained within the monumental Medici Chapels, in Michelangelo's New Sacristy (begun by the artist in 1520 and completed by Vasari in 1557), are the tombs of the Medici Princes, the great rulers of Florence. Carved by Michelangelo, the beautifully sculpted head of Giuliano, Duke of Nemours is illustrated right, and above right the statue representing Night, which, with the figure of Day, adorns the sarcophagus beneath the seated form of the Duke. Also by Michelangelo, the symbolic figure of Dawn above, with its complementary image of Dusk, graces the sarcophagus of the Tomb of Lorenzo, Duke of Urbino.

Displayed in the Museum Firenze Com'era, the painting depicting the 'Piazza Santa Croce during a Carnival' by Giovanni Signorini is shown overleaf above left, and below left 'The Voyage of the Three Kings' by Benozzo Gozzoli which is on view in the Medici-Riccardi Palace. An outstanding composition by Giorgio Vasari, 'The Doubting Thomas' overleaf right is one of the many fine works of art in the Church of Santa Croce.

One of Michelangelo's most emotive studies, the Pietà left is situated in the Cathedral of Santa Maria del Fiore and although unfinished at the time of the artist's death, was subsequently completed by Tiberio Calcagni.

Part of the magnificent Silver Reredos in the Museum of the Opera del Duomo, the detail above portrays the meeting between Christ and St. John the Baptist. Depicting the meeting between Solomon and Sheba, the detailed illustration right is one of ten gilt-bronze panels in the East Door (Gate of Paradise) below of the Baptistery and the work of Lorenzo Ghiberti.

Devoted to Fra. Angelico, the ancient Convent of San Marco, with its beautiful Library above left *containing fine codices, antiphonals and missals, exemplified above,* was rebuilt by Michelozzo in 1437, to the order of Cosimo the Elder. An example of Monastic architecture of the 16th century, its St. Antonino Cloister center right *is so called for the fresco paintings in the lunettes of the arcade that depict the life of the Saint, and* top *is shown the Crucifix with St. Dominic, by Fra. Angelico, which is sited on the wall opposite the Cloister entrance.*

Below left *can be seen the Cloister of San Lorenzo, and* below, *in the Medici Chapels at the rear of the Church, the magnificent dome frescoes in the Chapel of the Princes, painted by Benvenuti in 1828.* Top right *is shown the courtyard of the Bargello, and* bottom right *the courtyard of the Medici-Riccardi Palace.*

41

In a country that pays particular attention to the quality of food, and where even the smallest of bars provide excellent snacks to accompany a wide range of drinks, Florence is no exception, and from the ritziest restaurant to the humblest establishment, the service is fast, efficient and friendly.

*...tanding on the south side of the Loggia del
Mercato Nuovo these pages – a vast cornucopia
of souvenirs of every description – is the famous
bronze boar, 'Il Porcellino', bottom right a copy of
...acca's original in the Uffizi Gallery.*

Across the red-tiled roofs of Florence *previous page, which still retains a characteristically medieval appearance, the jumbled buildings, dotted with so many historical landmarks, give way to the rolling Tuscan hills punctuated by vineyards and orchards, villas and farms, that encircle this ancient city, lying almost at the center of the Italian peninsula.*

Around this fascinating city, newspaper stands, gaily festooned stalls and colorful street markets of every description, jostle for space amid the beautiful buildings that, enshrined with countless treasures, bear witness to the city's glorious past.

A proliferation of markets is shown on these pages, *and* overleaf *the excitement of an electric storm as it lights the night sky above the Tuscan hills and shadowy buildings on the banks of the Arno River.*

51

53

Housed in the magnificent Uffizi Gallery, with its outstanding collection of art masterpieces, the paintings displayed on these pages and overleaf are among the finest examples of Italian schools of art.

'Flora', a youthful composition by Titian, one of the greatest artists of the Renaissance and an influential figure in Western art, is shown above, and above left 'Rest on the Flight into Egypt', an early work by Correggio, a Renaissance painter of the Parma school, noted for his harmonious use of color and unified compositions.

Indicative of the highly original work of Caravaggio, whose technique of tenebrism (highly contrasted effects of light and shadow) added realism and drama to his paintings, is 'The Youthful Bacchus' below left, also an early work by this talented artist who played an important role in the development of Baroque painting.

'Portrait of a Princess of the Medici Family' below, and 'Lucrezia Panciatichi' right, one of a companion pair of panel portraits, are two fine examples of the Florentine Mannerist style of Agnolo Bronzino, a court painter to the Medici.

Characteristic of the work of Sandro Botticelli, 'The Birth of Venus' overleaf is synonymous with the spirit of the Renaissance era.

Further examples of the Uffizi Gallery's wide range of paintings are shown on these pages, overleaf and following pages, and include: 'The Ascension' above, part of a triptych by the first Renaissance artist of northern Italy, Andrea Mantegna; a detail from the 'Adoration of the Magi' above left by Gentile da Fabriano, an exponent of the Florid International Gothic style; 'Coronation of the Virgin' below left, 'Madonna and Child with Two Angels' below and 'Adoration of the Infant Jesus with St. Hilarius' above right, three outstanding compositions by the highly-gifted Fra. Filippo Lippi; 'Coronation of the Virgin' below right, combining both Gothic and Renaissance characteristics, by Fra. Angelico, and 'Primavera' ('Allegory of Spring') overleaf, another exquisite example of the work of Botticelli.

A youthful work, executed for the Church of San Bartolomeo di Monteoliveto, near Florence, 'The Annunciation' above reveals the scientific insight and harmony between figures and setting that mark the genius of Leonardo da Vinci, a man of exceptional talent who excelled not only in the field of painting, but also in the spheres of anatomy, sculpture, architecture and engineering.

Shown left is 'The Golden Age', an intricately detailed composition by Jacopo Zucchi; below 'The Madonna of the Goldfinch', one of the first of Raphael Santi's famed series of Madonna altarpieces which show his growing mastery of Leonardo's innovative 'sfumato' technique, and right 'Madonna Enthroned between two Angels', an outstanding example of the work of the Flemish artist Hans Memling, the leading painter of the Bruges school, demonstrating the calm idealism of his figures and faces imbued with a sweet and gentle piety.

63

Flowing along wide gravel beds, the Arno River, shown above and center right with the unique Ponte Vecchio, is not far from its source in the Appenines which lie beyond the crowded rooftops of the city left. Much of Florence's political history was made in the Piazza della Signoria, named for the 13th century fortified castle (Palazzo Vecchio) bottom right, that occupies one side of this ancient square, with its age-old monuments and impressive Neptune Fountain top right, created by Bartolomeo Ammanati.

Floodlit by night, the majestic Basilica of Santa Croce, one of the foremost Franciscan churches in Italy, can be seen below, and overleaf is a superb panorama of Florence from the terraces of the Piazzale Michelangelo.

Dramatic sunsets fill the sky and lend a special magic to this enchanting city – throwing into sharp relief the lighted lanterns on the banks of the silvery Arno left and the shadowy form of the Ponte S. Trinita above, while below an evening mist blots out the distant hills as night enfolds the city.

Sited close to the medieval walls which once surrounded the city, the floodlit church of San Frediano in Cestello, with its rough façade surmounted by a fine cupola, is shown right, mirrored in the river's dark and glassy surface.

Included in the magnificent statuary gracing the Loggia della Signoria are: left 'Perseus', Cellini's masterpiece; below 'The Rape of Polyxena' by Pio Fedi, and right Giambologna's 'Rape of the Sabines'.

The bronze statue of 'Mercury' by Giambologna, one of the many fine exhibits in the National Museum of the Bargello, is shown top; below left the Michelozzo Courtyard and its central fountain, surmounted by a copy of Verrochio's 'Winged Cupid with Dolphin', in the Palazzo Vecchio, and below the Tomb of Michelangelo, created by Vasari, within the Basilica of Santa Croce.

Within the magnificent Pitti Palace is the splendid Palatine Gallery, housing a large collection of works of art. The exquisite *Room of the Saturn* above, named after the frescoes on the ceiling by Ciro Ferri, contains paintings by many outstanding artists, while the *Green Room* left is noted for its superb Gobelin tapestries depicting *Stories of Esther*. Executed by Guido Reni, 'The Young Bacchus' is shown right; below *the 'Madonna of the Conception' by the great Venetian Mannerist painter Jacopo Tintoretto, and overleaf 'The Consequences of War', one of many mythological compositions by Peter Paul Rubens.*

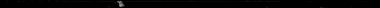

Displayed in the Palatine Gallery's Room of the
Education of Jupiter, 'Judith and Holofernes'
above far left, *the work of Cristofani Allori, a
painter of the late Florentine Mannerist school, i
considered to be the artist's masterpiece.*

The portrait of 'Eleonora de' Medici' above is
*indicative of the ornate, grandiose style of the
celebrated portraitist Frans Pourbus, who
produced many studies of the nobility.*

Contained in the Room of the Iliad, the portrait
'Waldemar Christian of Denmark' left is by
Justus Sustermans, *a noted portrait and figure
painter.*

Revealing the artistry of Bartolomé Esteban
Murillo, 'Madonna and Child' right, *can be seen
in the Gallery's Room of Mars, and below
'Madonna and Child', a devotional painting by
Carlo Dolci.*

'A View of the Coast of Naples from the Sea'
overleaf, above, *and 'The Convent of S. Paolo
Albano' overleaf, below, are two fine
compositions by the artist and draftsman Gaspa
van Wittel.*

Here, in the crowd-thronged Piazza della Signoria these pages, this graceful square dominated by the Palazzo Vecchio below and its slender tower which holds the city's first public clock, the history of Florence was forged, for it was here that her bitter internal struggles were fought and here that she affirmed her power and glory. Across the square, to the left of the Old Palace above, rises the bell-tower of the Badia Church, flanked by the Bargello to the right and the Duomo's Cupola to the left.

81

Finally completed by Emilio De Fabris in the late 19th century, the magnificent façade of the Cathedral of Sta. Maria del Fiore, a detail of which is shown overleaf left, is a triumph of Gothic splendor. Above the central door can be seen the beautiful mosaic left, surmounted by the sculpture groups below right that are placed in niches along the length of the façade, while below is featured the mosaic above the door to the left side of the Basilica.

Perched atop the superb dome above right, the white lantern top is also the work of Filippo Brunelleschi who began construction of the cupola, a masterpiece both technically and artistically, in 1420.

Set like a jewel against the verdant hills, the majestic Basilica is pictured overleaf right with the Bargello tower, and below are shown the exquisite mullioned windows of the Campanile.

The famous Bacchino Fountain above right, *said
to be a portrait of Cosimo I's dwarf, and
Buontalenti's Grotto, a fantastic creation of man-
made grottoes, frescoes, sculptures and fake
incrustations these pages, are located in the
delightful Boboli Gardens.
     Set amid the lush Tuscan landscape overleaf,
the Carthusian Monastery previous page is
perched on a cypress covered hill near Galluzzo,
some five km. from Florence.*

Converted to a museum after the suppression of the monastic orders in 1866, the Museum of San Marco, housed in an ancient 13th-century convent on the site of an old monastery of the Vallombrosian monks, is devoted to Fra. Angelico, whose gentleness and sensitivity is clearly discernible in his deeply compassionate compositions.

'The Last Supper', one of a cycle of thirty-five paintings for the door of a silver chest, is illustrated above; below 'The Crucifixion', and left the detail depicting the grieving Madonna 'Lamenting the Dead Christ'.

'The Last Judgement', one of numerous paintings on wood by Fra. Angelico, is contained within the adjacent Pilgrim's Hostel. Shown right is the upper section depicting Christ enthroned; overleaf the left-hand section denoting the righteous joining with the angels in a jubilant dance, and on page 96, the right-hand section portraying the descent of the condemned into hell's inferno.

First published 1979 by Colour Library International Ltd.
© 1979 Illustrations and text: Colour Library International Ltd., 163 East 64th St., New York, N.Y.10021.
Colour Separations by La Cromolito, Milan, Italy.
Display and text filmsetting by Focus Photoset, London, England.
Printed and bound by JISA-RIEUSSET, Barcelona, Spain.
All rights reserved.
ISBN 0-8317-3379-9 Library of Congress Catalogue Card No. 79-90598
Published in the United States of America by Mayflower Books, Inc., New York City.